100 TENNIS MANTRAS

By 61 Tennis Masters

Lukas Swift

100 TENNIS MANTRAS

Preface

A mantra can help you win a match. A good mantra can help you win a championship.

When everything is on the line, and emotions are running high, tennis becomes completely mental – and the player who will emerge victorious will be the one with the clearest head. At those key moments, having a safe phrase –a phrase that you can repeat over and over again in your mind– can quiet bad thoughts and make you focus on the point you are about to play.

In this book you will find one hundred mantras useful for different moments of your tennis journey. Some will help you prepare for a match, and some are ideal for the match itself, either when you are ahead and start to get a little tight or when you are behind and start (don't do it!) to give up. Others are intended for those moments when, already off the court, you must face victory or defeat with honesty and character.

Nobody knows more about tennis than the great tennis masters. That is why all these mantras are based on sayings and experiences of the greatest players, from retired legends (Arthur Ashe, Billie Jean King, Andre Agassi, Serena Williams) to the stars of the moment (Carlos Alcaraz, Iga Swiatek, Stefanos Tsitsipas, Nick Kyrgios) –and, of course, from the Big 3 themselves: Roger, Rafa and Novak.

Time!

1

You belong here

"I think luck falls on not just the brave but also the ones who believe they belong there."

– Novak Djokovic

2

Let the racket do the talking

"I'll let the racket do the talking."

– John McEnroe

3

Be grateful you are able to play

"Never take it for granted because soon enough it will be taken away. Time is tough. Every time you go out on the court be thankful. Be grateful. Believe me, I am. If you are lucky enough to be a tennis player you should recognize that it's a privilege to be able to walk out on that court and play the game."

– Brad Gilbert

4

Stop making excuses and start where you are

"Start where you are. Use what you have. Do what you can."

– Arthur Ashe

5

Your future needs you –your past doesn't

"At the end of the day, all you need is hope, persistence and strength. Your future needs you. Your past doesn't."

– Stefanos Tsitsipas

6

Go through the window while it is open

"Tennis is a small window. You are not going to have unlimited chances, unlimited opportunities. You can't waste time."

– Nick Kyrgios

7

Find your own path

"You have to find it. No one else can find it for you."

– Bjorn Borg

8

The tennis ball doesn't know who you are

"The tennis ball doesn't know how old I am. The ball doesn't know if I'm a man or a woman or if I come from a communist country or not. Sport has always broken down these barriers."

– Martina Navratilova

9

Put in what you want to get out

"Tennis is one of those sports: whatever you put in, you get out."

– Grigor Dimitrov

10

Practice the right way

"You can work really hard, but if you are not training in the right way, you are not going to improve and get to the level that you want to."

– Michael Chang

11

Keep working –because others are

"You have to continue working because everybody is. Once you stop, the others will overtake you."

– Dominic Thiem

12

Love the game

"I love the winning, I can take the losing, but most of all I love to play."

– Boris Becker

13

Respect the game

"Most players who play tennis love the game. But I think you also have to respect it. You want to do everything you can in your power to do your best. And for me, I know I get insane guilt if I go home at the end of the day and don't feel I've done everything I can. If I know I could have done something better, I have this uneasy feeling."

– Andy Roddick

14

Always look like a winner

"Regardless of how you feel inside, always try to look like a winner."

– Arthur Ashe

15

It's just you and me, baby

"People don't get it. They think that because tennis is played at these clubs that it's a rich man's sport. But it doesn't take more than a racket and a heart to play this game. That's the great thing about a sport like tennis. It's a great test of democracy in action. Me and you, man, in the arena. Just me and you, baby. Doesn't matter how much you have, or who your dad is, or if you went to Harvard, or Yale, or whatever. Just me and you."

– Pancho Segura

16

Embrace the hard work

"There is no way around the hard work. Embrace it. You have to put in the hours because there is always something you can improve. You have to put in a lot of sacrifice and effort for sometimes little reward but you have to know that, if you put in the right effort, the reward will come."

– Roger Federer

17

Enjoy the suffering

"I learned during all my career to enjoy the suffering."

– Rafael Nadal

18

Don't just play tennis –live tennis

"Tennis has to become everything to you if you are going to make it to the top. You have to live it."

– Monica Seles

19

Improve towards perfection, every day

"There is no such thing as perfection, only improvement."

– Jannik Sinner

20

Work on your foundation before adding ornaments

"It's so important to have a good foundation in everything, and after that, you can add complications and throw some more interesting things in."

– Emma Raducanu

21

Winning is just a bonus

"You just don't play tennis and win, no, it's not like that. You work hard to improve your skills. Then you play what you learned. Winning is just a bonus."

– Rafael Nadal

22

Acknowledge your nerves as something positive

"I get nervous every match, before the match especially. But I think it's a good sign. That means you want to win."

– Kei Nishikori

23

Go into each match believing you can beat every player

"You have to go into each match believing you can beat all of the players."

– Andy Murray

24

**Play a great first point –and then
a better second one**

"I played a great first point."

– Tin Henman
(after losing 6-0, 6-0 to Pete Sampras)

25

Play each point like your life depends on it

"I play each point like my life depends on it."

– Rafael Nadal

26

Be physically loose and mentally tight

"The ideal attitude is to be physically loose and mentally tight."

– Arthur Ashe

27

Enjoy yourself on court

"At the end of the day, I am playing tennis, a sport I love. If you are not enjoying yourself on court, you are lost."

– Carlos Alcaraz

28

Do not rush –tennis is long-distance

"Tennis is long-distance. You can't always race down the Autobahn at 220 km/h. You have to learn that sometimes 110 is enough."

– Brad Gilbert

29

The next point –that's all you must think about

"The next point –that's all you must think about."

– Rod Laver

30

As long as you are playing, you have a chance

"The great part about tennis is you can't run out the clock... As long as we were still playing, I had a chance."

– Andre Agassi

31

Lose your fear of losing

"Losing is not my enemy, fear of losing is my enemy."

– Rafael Nadal

32

Think positive –even when you miss

"If you win it or you lose it, after the point you have the chance to think about it in a positive way."

– Carlos Alcaraz

33

Play the ball, not the opponent

"I told myself to play free. You play the ball. You don't play the opponent. Be free in your head. Be free in your shots. Go for it. The brave will be rewarded here."

– Roger Federer

34

Beat the strongest with your mind

"I didn't have the same fitness or ability as the other girls, so I had to beat them with my mind."

– Martina Hingis

35

Your serve is only yours

"The serve is the only thing you know about yourself when you play tennis. If you make it right, you make it right. Nobody can touch you when you serve. Nobody can disturb you. You have the ball in the hand."

– Jo-Wilfried Tsonga

36

Ace in the most important moments

"The difference between me and Guy Forget? He had aces on 15-0, I on 30-40."

– Boris Becker

37

Be ready for the unknown

"The service is a window into the unknown."

– Lars Gustafsson

38

Dictate the point after the serve

"Serving plays an important role on any surface. You have to understand that next shot after the serve you have to lead the game."

– Daniil Medvedev

39

Be Tom, not Jerry

"I used to pretend that I was Tom attacking Jerry – who was drawn on the ball."

– Monica Seles

40

Have fun –tennis is a game

"I think, for me, I just really want to have fun with every match that I play because tennis is a game."

– Naomi Osaka

41

Smile

"When I smile play my best tennis."

– Ons Jabeur

42

There's always some space to put the ball in

"Anyone who has ever played tennis knows that the court is pretty big and you always have some space to put the ball in."

– Tomas Berdych

43

Be patient –the ball is round and the game is long

"The ball is round, the game is long."

– Bjorn Borg

44

Fight like an animal fighting for its life

"Tennis players we are always playing in center courts that feel like arenas. And when we get on the court and the crowd cheers your name or salutes you –it's like you are a gladiator in the arena. And everyone is cheering – and you are fighting, you are screaming, during your strokes. It feels like you are an animal, fighting for your life."

– Novak Djokovic

45

Be glad you are not playing against yourself

"I'm glad I don't have myself as opponent –today I feel so fit!"

– Fred Perry

46

Silent your cell phone

"I was playing in the juniors at Wimbledon, and I forgot to turn my mobile phone off. It was lying there in my bag and it rang in the middle of a match, and it was one of my friends from school saying, 'Murray, you're on the telly!' I learnt from that. I now put my phone on silent."

– Andy Murray

47

Stop thinking and start feeling

"Freed from the thoughts of winning, I instantly play better. I stop thinking, start feeling. My shots become a half-second quicker, my decisions become the product of instinct rather than logic."

– Andre Agassi

48

No drama, please

"It's not an opera, it's a game."

– Ilie Nastase

49

Give everything you have

"I think my greatest victory was every time I walked out there, I gave it everything I had. I left everything out there. That's what I'm most proud of."

– Jimmy Connors

50

Pressure is a privilege –earn it

"Pressure is a privilege. It only comes to those who earn it."

– Billy Jean King

51

Raise your level –and maintain it

"The difference of great players is at a certain point in a match they raise their level of play and maintain it. Lesser players play great for a set, but then less."

– Pete Sampras

52

Grow your brain

"I believe the brain is like a muscle –like any other it can be improved."

– Ivan Lendl

53

Accept the stress –and deal with it

"Stress is part of your career. You have to accept it and deal with it because there is a lot of emotion in tennis."

– Stan Wawrinka

54

Take advantage of the opportunities you have created

"Tennis is basically a game where you try to create an opportunity for yourself to finish the point, because you can't wait for the opponent to miss anymore. Well, if you create an opportunity and don't take advantage of it, you let the opponent back to even, then you are just starting the point over, so you have to take advantage of them."

– Ivan Lendl

55

Go for the fence with no regret

"I go for my shots with no regret, even if I play to the fence."

– Garbine Muguruza

56

Hate losing even more than you love winning

"I hate to lose more than I love to win. I can't bear to see the slightest sign of satisfaction on my opponent's face."

– Jimmy Connors

57

Win the inner game

"In tennis, victory is not played between two lines but between the two ears of the player."

– Novak Djokovic

58

Crush those thoughts

"Because what I battle hardest to do in a tennis match is to quiet the voices in my head, to shut everything out of my mind but the contest itself and concentrate every atom of my being on the point I am playing. If I made a mistake on a previous point, forget it; should a thought of victory suggest itself, crush it."

– Rafael Nadal

59

Just be better than the other guy

"You don't have to be the best in the world every time you go out there. You just have to be better than one guy."

– Andre Agassi

60

Have fun while being serious

"I have that balance of having fun –because I can need to have a ton of fun– but also locking it in at times."

– Frances Tiafoe

61

Overpower, overtake, overcome

"Overpower. Overtake. Overcome."

– Serena Williams

62

Take the initiative and play your game

"You've got to take the initiative and play your game. In a decisive set, confidence is the difference."

– Chris Evert

63

Concentrate on concentrating

"I just try to concentrate on concentrating."

– Martina Navratilova

64

Know your strengths

"My greatest strength is consistency."

– Daniil Medvedev

65

Be smart

"My coach told me to play smarter. That's just not my game."

– Marat Safin

66

Double down when you are ahead

"The time your game is most vulnerable is when you're ahead; never let up."

– Rod Laver

67

You don't change a winning tactic

"You don't change a winning tactic."

– Patrice Dominguez

68

Fight just one opponent

"My problem is that in each match I have to fight against five opponents: the official, the public, the ball boys, the net, and myself. That's why my mind is sometimes somewhere else."

– Goran Ivanisevic

69

Enjoy the big matches

"Beating someone 6-2, 6-2 is fun, but going 7-6 in the fifth set after almost five hours of play is better."

– Jimmy Connors

70

The big matches –that's why you play tennis

"Those big matches, when you go through so much, are the best thing. Those matches are why you play tennis."

– Stan Wawrinka

71

Never sink into your opponent's level

"A mediocre player sinks to the level of his opponent."

– Raúl Ramírez

72

Accept that you won't always play your best tennis

"Sometimes you're looking to play perfect tennis but it's not going to happen all the time and you have to accept it."

– Andy Murray

73

**Grit your teeth and find a way
when you are not playing your best tennis**

"That's when you've got to grit your teeth and hang in there and try and find a way to win when you're not playing your best tennis –that's what I can be proud of".

– Lleyton Hewitt

74

Disguise your weaknesses

"During a match, you are in a permanent battle to fight back your everyday vulnerabilities, bottle up your human feelings. It's a kind of self-hypnosis, a game you play, with deadly seriousness, to disguise your own weaknesses from yourself, as well as from your rival."

– Rafael Nadal

75

Believe in victory more than your opponent

"The winner is the one who believes in victory more."

– Novak Djokovic

76

Carry yourself with pride –even when you lose

"Sportsmanship for me is when a guy walks off the court and you really can't tell whether he won or lost, when he carries himself with pride either way."

– Jim Courier

77

Give your opponent a hug

"When the last point is done, we are humans. Give your opponent a hug and say, 'Great fight', and that's all."

– Novak Djokovic

78

Get some rest

"My favorite surface is my bed".

– Jim Courier

79

Have a short memory

"Every good tennis player has to have a short memory. Good or bad."

– Alexander Zverev

80

Recover after every fall

"I really think a champion is defined not by their wins but by how they can recover when they fall."

– Serena Williams

81

Focus on the process

"I have learned to not look so much at the results and tune out the outside pressures. It has taken a lot of work and I am still growing and learning how to do that, but focusing on the process, trying to relax as much as possible and just have fun has always produced some of my best tennis."

– Coco Gauff

82

Don't just win –improve

"If you win without progressing, you will never be a champion."

– John McEnroe

83

Character is built through adversity

"If everything was going smoothly, you would never build character."

– María Sharapova

84

Tennis can give you soul

"Tennis has given me soul."

– Martina Navratilova

85

Learn to be disciplined

"You will never be always motivated so you must learn to be disciplined."

– Iga Swiatek

86

Never look back –look forward

"I never look back; I look forward."

– Steffi Graf

87

Have a talented life –so you can be a talented player

"Everybody talks about talent. But talent is not only athleticism. It's not only tennis shots. It's everything. It's the attitude you have about life."

– Gael Monfils

88

Do not compare yourself to others

"I think to compare yourself and your results against anyone is probably like the thief of happiness."

– Emma Raducanu

89

Don't forget you are alive

"My motto is: I'm alive, so that means I can do anything."

– Venus Williams

90

There is no shortcuts in tennis

"There is no shortcuts. Play your best tennis, give your heart out, and anything can happen."

– Grigor Dimitrov

91

Keep trying –and then keep trying some more

"With a defeat, when you lose, you get up, you make it better, and you try again. That's what I do in life, when I get down, when I get sick, I don't want to just stop. I keep going, and I try to do more. Everyone always says never give up, but you really have to take that to heart and really do never definitely give up. Keep trying."

– Serena Williams

92

Turn your defeat into research

"For me losing a tennis match isn't a failure, it's research."

– Billie Jean King

93

Quit once and you will keep twice –and more

"If you quit once, it's so much easier to quit the second, third, fourth time."

– Michael Chang

94

You are who you are –and that's okay

"Sometimes I wish I could have been a bit more relaxed, but then I wouldn't have been the same player."

– Steffi Graff

95

Keep playing until you get it right

"Champions keep playing until they get it right."

– Billie Jean King

96

Have faith –even on the edge of the precipice

"It's on the edge of the precipice where, all of a sudden, something happens."

– Arnaud Boetsch

97

Do it your way

"There's no right way, there's no wrong way, there's just my way."

– Ash Barty

98

Nobody beats you 17 times in a row

"Let that be a lesson to you all: nobody –nobody– beats Vitas Gerulaitis 17 times in a row".

– Vitas Gerulaitis

99

At the end of the day, tennis is tennis

"After almost 30 years of playing this sport, I've learned something. I've learned that, no matter what happens, or happened... or where you are, or where you've been... at the end of the day: tennis is tennis. It's always, always tennis. And there's nothing better."

– Venus Williams

100

Play and play and play some more

"The only possible regret I have is the feeling that I will die without playing enough tennis."

– Jean Borotra